Toe Shoes and Tutus

by Paul Meeks ❖ illustrated by E. Velasquez

Harcourt

Orlando   Boston   Dallas   Chicago   San Diego

Visit *The Learning Site!*

www.harcourtschool.com

Ballet has been popular for many years. It is an ever-changing art form. The ballet we know today is very different from the ballet that began in Italy in the 1500s. For example, then all ballet dancers were men. Women had to devote all of their time to their families.

Today, ballet dancers dance to the music of large orchestras. Back then, the music was much more simple. The only instruments played were reeds and pipes. Ballets were performed only in palaces, rather than on stage in a theater. Because of this, common people and migrant workers could not attend the ballet. The men danced in rows, moving slowly to the music.

Many people think ballet began in France. However, ballet began in Italy and was brought to France in the mid-1500s by Catherine de Médici. After she married Henry II of France and became queen, she missed the ballet. Queen Catherine had dancers come from Italy to dance for her in the palace in Paris. During the next 200 years, ballet thrived in France.

In the late 1600s, ballet began to change. King Louis XIV of France started the first school of dancing in France. It was called the Royal Academy of Dancing and Music. King Louis gave women the chance to study dancing, and they danced in the ballets at his court. Common people could enjoy ballet now, too. Students from the school also danced at public theaters.

Today, all the ballet positions, steps, and jumps have French names. This happened because French ballet teachers were invited to teach in other countries. They always taught in their own language, no matter what country they were in.

The steps of dancers in the past were not as difficult as those of dancers today. That is because female dancers wore everyday clothes when they danced. These clothes included tight corsets and long dresses that extended to the dancers' feet. These dancers also wore shoes with heels.

Marie Camargo (1710–1770), the first great French ballerina, was not exactly timid. She was the first to cut her dress a few inches shorter and remove the heels from her shoes. This allowed her to dance fast steps more easily. Later, other dancers also wore shorter dresses and shoes without heels. These new clothing styles helped the dancers to more easily do fancy steps, jumps, and turns.

The first ballerina to dance en pointe, or on the points of her ballet slippers, was Marie Taglioni (1804–1884). She was also the first dancer to wear a tutu. In her day, the tutu was long. It was made of many layers, so that the skirt would be shaped like a bell or an upside-down flower. The ballets from Taglioni's time are known as "romantic" or "white" ballets.

Male ballet dancers do not dance on their toes. Some lift the female dancers high in the air and hold them as they take their difficult poses. Dancers are also trained to spin and to make leaps and turns in the air. All dancers must be very strong and must do a lot of training and exercise to keep their bodies healthy.

Classical ballet was created in Russia. It is a combination of the French style (delicate poses and dainty steps) and the Italian style (high jumps and difficult turns).

The Russians also created the classic tutu. This skirt is very short. It allows greater flexibility because it leaves the dancers' legs free.

One of the most famous Russian dancers
was Anna Pavlova (1882–1931). Anna
attended the Russian Imperial School of
Ballet. It offered a scholarship to all students
who passed the entrance exam.

In 1905, Pavlova danced her famous three-
minute solo, The Dying Swan. Her costume
was partly covered with real feathers.

Another famous Russian dancer was a man named Vaslav Nijinsky (1890–1950), who was one of Pavlova's partners. He could leap very high into the air. He is still remembered for his amazing jumps. Once, when asked how he jumped so high, he said, "It is quite easy—you have merely to pause a little in the air and then come down again." The trick of how to "pause a little in the air" remains a mystery.

1

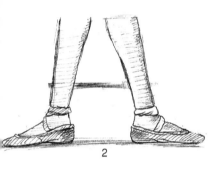

2

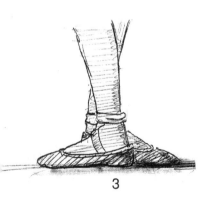

3

Classical ballet is based on five foot positions. Almost all ballet steps begin and end with one of the five foot positions. These five positions are among the first things a ballet student learns.

In first position, the heels are together, with toes opened out to each side.

Second position is like first position. The only difference is that the feet are spread apart the length of one's own foot. The heels are no longer touching.

In third position, the front foot is placed with the heel touching the instep of the back foot.

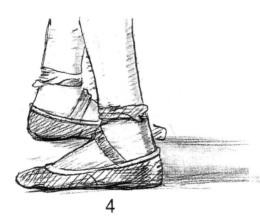

4

5

In fourth position, the heel of the front foot is opposite the toe of the back foot. The feet are parallel and separated by the length of one's own foot.

In fifth position, the feet are close together, with the heel of the front foot touching the toe of the back foot.

In all positions, the weight is placed evenly on both feet. The knees are not bent, and the legs and feet are turned out.

After the time of Pavlova and Nijinsky, ballet began to change. Dancers and choreographers found that the few positions used in classical ballet were not enough to express the emotions they wanted to show on stage. They wanted to be able to move more freely. They also wanted greater variety in costumes. They were not too timid to dance barefoot or in sandals, or to wear costumes other than toe shoes and tutus.

Sometimes, dancers wanted to express a mood rather than tell a story as in clas- sical ballet. That is how modern bal- let developed. This newer style has thrived in recent years.

A young apprentice today begins by studying the classical style. It is still thought to be the best way to train the body for ballet. Even modern prima ballerina Evelyn Cisneros, grand-daughter of Hispanic migrant workers, started with the first five positions of the feet, just as Marie Camargo did in the 1700s. By practicing these positions, she earned a scholarship to the San Francisco Ballet School. She went on to become a very famous American ballerina.